COMMERCIAL CULTURE in China
中国商务文化

U0955547

COMMERCIAL SOCIALIZING
商务社交

《中国商务文化》编写组

北京语言大学出版社
BEIJING LANGUAGE AND CULTURE UNIVERSITY PRESS
中央广播电视大学音像出版社
MULTIMEDIA PRESS, OPEN UNIVERSITY OF CHINA

总 监 制：戚德祥　梁小庆

监　　制：张　健　魏　捷

顾　　问：周小华

主　　编：李孚嘉

编　　者：李佳琳　唐琪佳　王　立　王墨妍　张维嘉
（按音序排列）

英文翻译：巩　熠　罗正鹏　孙齐圣

英文审定：【美】Andrew Bauer　李亚婉

目 录 CONTENTS

共事原则
ESSENTIAL PRINCIPLES

　　一位在中国经商多年的澳大利亚商人总结他的经验时说：“重要的不是你的专业知识，而是你认识谁。”“你认识谁”指的是你拥有的“关系”，在中国经商办事，关系非常重要。

An Australian merchant who has been doing business in China for many years summarized his experience as follows: “It’s not important what you know, but who you know.” “Who you know" refers to the *guanxi* (personal relationships or connections) that you have. *Guanxi* is extremely important for doing business and handling affairs in China.

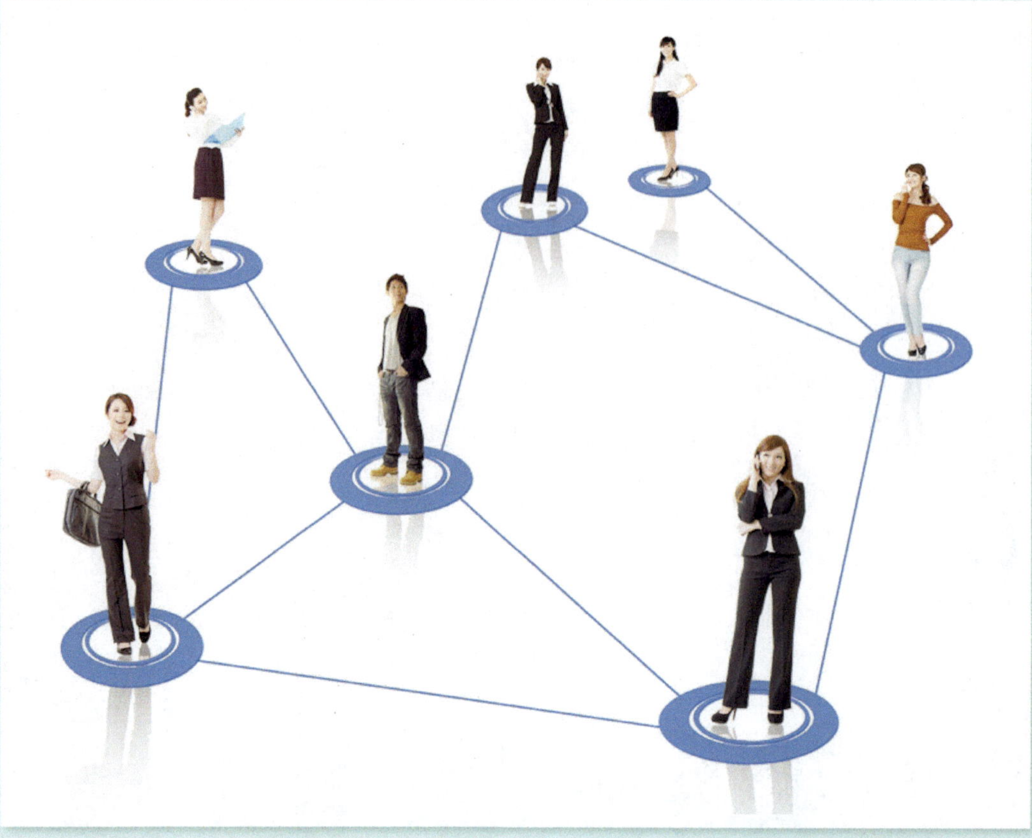

与中国人进行商务合作，总的共事原则离不开“关系”二字。“关系”广泛地讲是指人际关系，是人与人之间通过交往和联系形成的一种心理连接。在中国，“关系”是一种很普遍的社会现象，它渗透到政治、经济、文化、生活等各个领域。中国人从生老病死、婚葬嫁娶，一直到衣食住行、文化娱乐，无不生活在巨大的关系网中。

在中国，为什么关系如此重要呢？这是因为，中国人的人际关系以人伦为中心，人情是维系人际关系的纽带。在古代，维系中国社会的主要经济活动是农业生产，因此家庭是最基本的社会单位。个人随着家人在固定的土地上从事生产，生于斯，长于斯，工作于斯，也终老于斯；日常生活中经常接触的人，除了家人便是亲戚、街坊邻里。在这样的社会背景下，中国人以儒家理论为基础，发展出一套以“情”为中心的行为规范：个人

When making business cooperation with Chinese, the general principle is inseparable from the two characters "*guanxi*". Broadly speaking, "*guanxi*" refers to interpersonal relationships, a kind of psychological connection formed among individuals who interact and communicate with each other. In China, "*guanxi*" is a very common social phenomenon penetrating into all domains such as politics, economy, culture, and life, etc. Ranging from birth, senility, illness, death, wedding and funeral to clothing, food, accommodation, transportation, culture and entertainment, Chinese people are invariably living in a huge network of "*guanxi*".

Why is *guanxi* so important in China? This is because the interpersonal relationship among Chinese centers on ethics, and human feelings are the bonds maintaining interpersonal relationships. In ancient times, the major economic activity holding Chinese society together was agricultural production, therefore a family was the most basic unit of society. Individuals, together with their family members, were engaged in the production process on a piece of fixed land. They were born there, lived there, grew up there, worked there, aged and died there. Apart from their family members, the people with whom they had frequent contact were their relatives or neighbors who lived nearby. In such a social context, Chinese people, based on the Confucian theory, developed a code of conduct centering on "feelings": individuals have to show "family affection" towards their own family members, and speak of "mutual favors" to close friends apart from their family members. They can, however, ignore all these things when dealing with unrelated strangers. Therefore, for Chinese people, if an individual is the core of concentric circles, the immediate layer surrounding the core involves family members, the layer outside family members includes people who are attached to the

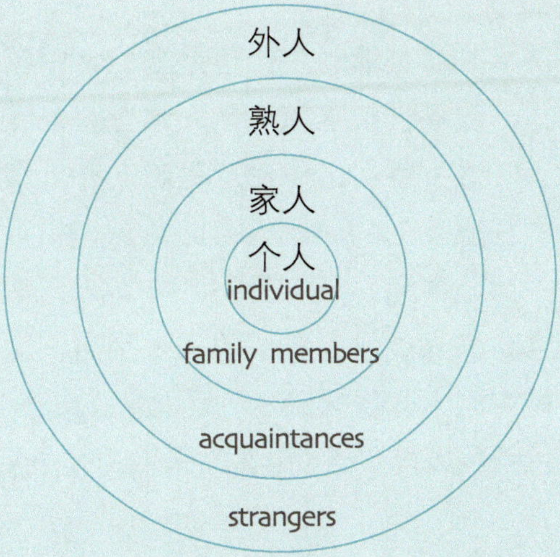

必须和家人讲“亲情”，和家庭以外的熟人讲“人情”，和自己不相干的陌生人，则不必讲究这些。因此，对于中国人来说，个人如果是同心圆的核心，外面便围绕着家庭成员，家人外围是和自己有关系的人，再外层就是和自己无关的陌生人了。而个人和这些不同圈子里的人交往，要采取不同的交往法则。

在商务活动中，也是如此，中国人一般习惯和家人、熟人这些“自己人”做生意。这种生意是建立在人情的基础之上的，他们彼此熟识，相互关照，讲究回报。另外，中国人还常常与家人或熟人介绍的人做生意，这是中国人降低风险的一种办法。与有关系的人打交道，中国人采取的是“人情法则”，主要通过人情、信任而不是契约来约束双方，因为“关系”意味着信任和忠诚。而在关系圈之外的人，也就是和自己没有关系的陌生人，是需要小心地开展合作关系的。与没有关系的陌生人打交道，中国人采取的是“公平法则”——不太讲人情，主要通过契约来约束双方，在具体的合作方法、利益分配等方面是严格依照契约办事的。

在中国，商务关系的一大特点就是倾向于长期合作。中国人不惜花很多时间、很多精力与你拉关系，甚至聊一些与生意无关的话题或者安排一些与生意无关的活动，这些都是他们希望与你建立关系的表现。为了保持长期合作，他们甚至会在一单生意结束后，继续花时间和精力去维护双方的关系。可以说，一旦关系建立起来，中国人便会表现出极大的忠诚和奉献精神，因此，他们认为花费再多的时间和精力去建立和维护关系都是值得的。

可见，在中国经商，需要先搞好关系，然后才能做好生意。

individual and the further distant circle pertains to unrelated strangers. To interact with people from all these different circles, a person should adopt different methods of interaction.

This is also true in business activities where Chinese people are generally accustomed to trade with their insiders such as families and acquaintances. This kind of business is established on the basis of personal relations among people who are familiar with each other, who care for each other and who value mutual returns as forms of reciprocal favors. In addition, Chinese people often do business with people who are introduced to them by family members or acquaintances, which is another way for Chinese to reduce risk. When dealing with people who are related to them, Chinese people opt for a "law of human relations" which binds people by personal connections and trust instead of by contracts, for "*guanxi*" means trust and loyalty. However, it's necessary to exercise caution when carrying out cooperation with people who are outside one's *guanxi* circle, namely unrelated strangers. When dealing with unrelated strangers who have no *guanxi* with them, Chinese people adopt a "law of fairness", which does not value much about personal relations but binds the two parties through contracts. In terms of specific methods for cooperation and distribution of benefits, they act strictly in accordance with the contracts.

In China, a prominent feature of business relations is their obvious long-term orientation. Chinese people will not regret over the considerable amount of time and energy spent in building *guanxi*; they even talk about topics irrelevant to business or arrange activities unrelated to business. These are all manifestations of their hope to establish *guanxi* with you. In order to keep long-term cooperation, they may even continue to spend time and energy in maintaining the *guanxi* between the two parties after a single trade is over. It can be said that once *guanxi* is established, Chinese people will show great loyalty and dedication. Therefore, they think it is worthwhile to spend as much time and effort as possible to build and maintain *guanxi*.

So we can see, to do business in China, one has to build good *guanxi*. Only after this one can succeed in doing business.

案例

Nicolas 就职于一家中国公司的人力资源部门。一次，领导希望全面改善一下公司岗位设置，特意派 Nicolas 去跟一家西班牙知名咨询公司洽谈。西班牙咨询公司给出了中肯的建议，却要价不菲。Nicolas 为了帮公司节省一笔费用，四处打听，终于找到另一家咨询公司，他们愿意以比西班牙咨询公司便宜三分之一的价格完善后续方案。Nicolas 马上把这个好消息告诉了领导。领导听后，语重心长地告诉 Nicolas："我们与这家西班牙咨询公司有 20 年的生意关系了，我们信得过这家公司，也绝不会为了一点儿小钱轻易更换我们的合作伙伴。" Nicolas 不明白，为什么一贯提倡节约生产经营成本的领导，这次却宁可多花钱也要找这家西班牙公司。

点评 Nicolas 看重的是眼前的利益，而领导更看重人情和长远利益，一旦关系建立起来，中国人便会表现出极大的忠诚和奉献精神。

行动指南

- 在中国，如果想办事比较顺利，不妨好好利用你在中国建立的同事关系、客户关系、朋友关系等，他们常常会很热心地帮助你。
- 如果你想利用第三方的关系为合作加分，一定要事先了解合作伙伴与第三方之间的实际关系如何。如果合作伙伴与第三方关系很好，你会收到预料的效果；反之，则会为你减分。

CASE STUDY

Nicolas is working in the human resource department of a Chinese company. Once, the leader of the company hoped to make an overall improvement to the arrangement of posts in the company and specifically sent Nicolas to negotiate with a well-known Spanish consulting firm. The Spanish consulting firm proposed pertinent suggestions, but asked for a large sum of money. To help the company save a sum of money, Nicolas inquired here and there and finally found another consulting firm willing to improve the follow-up program at one third the price of the Spanish consulting firm. Nicolas immediately told the good news to the company leader. Upon hearing the news, the leader told Nicolas in sincere and meaningful words "we have been doing business for 20 years with the Spanish consulting firm. We believe in this company and will never change our cooperators for the sake of a small sum of money". Nicolas didn't understand why his leader who had always advocated the saving of production and operation costs would rather spend more money this time in order to choose the expensive Spanish company.

Comments: Whereas Nicolas values the immediate benefits, Chinese people emphasize more human relations and long-term benefits. Once *guanxi* has been established, Chinese people will show great loyalty and dedication.

ADVICE

- In China, if you want to work more smoothly, you may wish to make good use of your established *guanxi* between colleagues, customers, friends, etc. They will usually be very glad to help you.

- If you want to make use of the *guanxi* of a third party in order to facilitate cooperation, you have to know the actual condition of *guanxi* between your cooperator and the third party. If your cooperator has a good *guanxi* with the third party, you will achieve the expected results. Otherwise, it will bring you more losses than gains.

建立关系

MAKING INITIAL CONTACT

澳大利亚商人 Darid Trethewey 曾说："这是中国，总之什么都没有建立关系那么重要！"那么，如何才能顺利地建立关系呢？

An Australian businessman once said,"This is in China. In short, nothing is as important as establishing *guanxi* (personal relationships or connections)!" How can we successfully establish *guanxi*, then?

在中国，关系很重要，人们不但在日常生活中讲关系，而且在政治和经济生活中也讲关系，关系成为了一种人们之间相互信任与合作的资源。

一个人建立的关系越多，认识的人就越多，在办事过程中就越容易找到有效的方法或途径，越容易找到自己所需要的资源所在，并且有越多人帮助自己获得这些资源，也越容易获得有利于自己发展的机会。相对于陌生人而言，人们更愿意向自己认识的人，尤其是关系较好的人寻求帮助，也更倾向于帮助自己认识的人和关系好的人。现在，中国人也把这种人际关系网络称为“人脉”。一个人脉广、关系网通达的人会被认为是有影响力和有背景的能人。

如何才能顺利地建立关系呢？

先要创造接触机会。建立关系的第一步是想办法接近你的合作人，如果合作人并不认识你，且他的级别又较高，你直接自荐很有可能被拒绝。因为中国人一般认为在正式做生意前，需要先与合作人建立信任的关系基础，贸然造访，没有信任基础，中国人一般很难马上接纳你。可以先通过合作人关系圈里的其他人引见，安排与合作人见面，这种认识的方式比较自然，成功的几率也更大。

接触之后，要尽快引起共鸣，也就是要想办法“拉关系”，借此拉近距离、巩固信任基础。比如，如果双方有相同的志向、信仰或兴趣，便会视为知己，畅所欲言。心理距离近了，

Guanxi plays an extremely important role in China. Chinese people not only stress *Guanxi* in their daily life but also in political and economic life. *Guanxi* has become a kind of resource for creating mutual trust and cooperation among people.

The more Guanxi a person establishes and the more people he/she is acquainted with, the easier he/she will find it to come up with effective solutions or methods in his/her matter dealing process and find where the resources he/she needs to acquire reside; besides, as more people are assisting him/her to obtain these resources, he/she will get more opportunities beneficial for self-development without much effort. Compared with strangers, Chinese are more inclined to seek help from people they know, especially those who have a close relationship with them. Similarly, Chinese tend to help people whom they know and those who are close to them. Now, Chinese people also refer to this network of interpersonal relationship as "renmai". Someone who has a wide renmai and powerful *Guanxi* network is regarded as a capable, influential individual with good background.

How can we successfully establish *Guanxi*?

First, create opportunities for contact. The first step toward establishing *Guanxi* is finding ways to approach your prospective cooperator. If the cooperator doesn't know you, plus he/she enjoys a superior social rank, your direct self-recommendation is very likely to be declined. Chinese people generally agree that it's necessary to build trust — the basis for personal relationships, with their prospective cooperators before formal business dealings take place. Chinese people usually find it difficult to accept someone who abruptly approaches them without the foundation of trust. Therefore, you can first of all seek introduction to your prospective cooperator from other people within his/her *Guanxi* network and then arrange an appointment with your cooperator. This way of getting to know people is more natural and brings about greater probability for a successful appointment.

After the initial contact with your cooperator, you should arouse a sense of resonance with him/her as soon as possible. This means you should think of ways to "pull *Guanxi* closer" in order to reduce the distance between you and your cooperator and

合作也会更加顺利。

见面之后还要持续交往沟通。在中国，商务宴请是最传统的商务交往模式。随着社会的发展，一些新的方式逐渐出现，除了参与高尔夫球、赛车俱乐部等高消费的群体体育运动外，在商务会馆聚会，一起去做桑拿，或者参加各类高管培训班都成为商务交往的重要途径和方式。

仅有吃喝玩乐是不够的，关键还要把合作人当成真正的朋友，去关心他、帮助他，为他提供实际价值，这样才能建立彼此牢不可破的关系。中国人重感情，有时候价格、品质、效率、规模等等都敌不过关怀的威力，一旦合作人认定你是真正关心他和他的处境，他就可能会与你合作。

值得注意的是，中国人在建立关系时，“公私”的界限比较模糊，他们更重视在公司框架下的人与人之间的私交。他们建立商务关系时常常会涉及有关人员的家人或私人朋友，人们会通过各种亲属、朋友的渠道积极主动地互相介绍和推荐。

建立良好的关系能让你从中受益匪浅，就像Juan Antonio Fernandez & Lauiie Underwood在他们的书《中国首席执行官》中所说的：“一旦生意关系建立，中国人倾向于表现出比发达国家标准来说更多的忠诚和奉献。”

consolidate the foundation for mutual trust. For instance, if the two parties cooperating with each other share the same pursuit, belief or interest, they will regard each other as confidant and speak their minds freely. Once people are psychologically closer to each other, the cooperation between them will be smoother.

People should keep in contact and go on communicating with each other after their first meeting. In China, business dinner is the most traditional mode of commercial exchanges. With the development of the society, a number of new forms gradually emerge. Apart from participating in such high consumption group sports as golf, racing clubs, etc., holding parties at business clubs, going to the sauna together or taking various kinds of training courses for senior executives are things that have invariably become important ways and methods for business exchange activities.

However, mere eating, drinking and entertainment are not sufficient. The key point is to regard one's cooperators as true friends, and care for them, help them and offer them real value. Only by doing this can we establish unbreakable relationships among the cooperating parties. Chinese people place much emphasis on emotion, thus sometimes the power of friendship outweighs such aspects as price, quality, productivity and scale. Once a cooperator is convinced of your genuine care for himself or his situation, he is likely to ignore some details and cooperate with you.

It is noteworthy that the boundary between "public and private" is rather vague when Chinese people establish *Guanxi* with each other for they emphasize more the personal relationships among people under the company framework. Among Chinese, the process of establishing business relationships often concerns family members or friends of the relevant individuals, and people would actively introduce or recommend each other through channels provided by various relatives and friends.

Establishing good relationships can benefit you a lot. Just as Juan Antonio Fernandez & Lauiie Underwood put in their book *China CEO: Voices of Experience from 20 International Business Leaders*: "As long as the business partnership is established, Chinese people tend to show higher levels of loyalty and dedication than the standards in developed countries".

案例

中国某大型公司招标合作伙伴，两家实力相当的外国公司得知这个消息后，先后赴中国洽谈合作事宜。A 公司事前经过精心准备，安排了满满一天的会议，上午是介绍公司的历史和业绩，下午和晚上是讨论具体合作方案，第二天一早就急匆匆回国去了。B 公司在中国待了整整一个星期，除了讨论协商具体方案外，还陪中方参加了一些商务社交活动，打打高尔夫球、做做桑拿、去商务会馆喝喝下午茶……增加了相互的了解。最后，B 公司成功中标。

点评 在实力等客观条件相差并不悬殊的情况下，“关系”往往会成为作决策的决定性因素。商务社交活动不止是娱乐，更是双方建立关系的重要环节，在这些交往中，能够进一步相互交流需求、沟通合作意向，更重要的是，可以获得中国人的信任。虽然 A 公司在具体的项目上也下了很多功夫，但没有留出时间让双方增进了解、拉近关系，而让与此相反的 B 公司赢得了机会。

行动指南

- 与中国人做生意，要重视在会场外下功夫，很多重要的决定往往是在会议之外作出的。
- 与中国人建立关系，必须要有耐心、恒心、信心，还要细心。

CASE STUDY

A large Chinese company is inviting bids from prospective cooperators. Upon learning the news, a powerful American enterprise and a relatively renowned French company arrive in China one after another to discuss affairs concerning the cooperation. The American enterprise is elaborately prepared in advance and arranges a whole day full of meetings, introducing its history and achievements in the morning and discussing the specific cooperation plan in the afternoon and evening. After that, the enterprise hurries back to America in the early morning on the next day. The French company, however, stays in China for a whole week. Though there is no fixed agenda for each day, they arranged some important business events with the Chinese counterpart. Apart from that, they arranged some social events such as playing golf, going to the sauna or drinking tea together at a business club .... The French company wins the bid.

Comments: Although the American enterprise is very powerful, it is not as good at establishing guanxi with the Chinese counterpart. It withdraws too hastily before the Chinese company establishes trust in it. Despite its disadvantage in strength compared with the American enterprise, the French company well understands how to build guanxi with its Chinese partner. Besides, it makes use of the business events to get to know the needs of the Chinese partner and negotiates mutual intentions for cooperation, thus gradually gaining the trust of the Chinese company and finally winning the opportunity.

ADVICE

- When doing business with Chinese, pay attention to efforts made outside the meeting room, for many important decisions are often made outside the meeting.
- To establish *guanxi* with Chinese, one must have patience, perseverance, confidence and attentiveness.

维护关系

MAINTAINING RELATIONSHIP

从 20 世纪 80 年代至今，越来越多的学术研究集中于中国的经济改革和发展，中国词汇“*guanxi*（关系）”频频出现在西方商业实务及学术杂志中。学者 Stone 总结道：“在中国如果没有关系，你将不可能生存！外国谈判者如果能够了解游戏规则，丰硕的成果会随之而来。”在中国，关系如此重要，如何才能维护好关系呢？

From the 1980s to present, more and more academic researches are concentrating on the reform and development of the Chinese economy. The Chinese word "*guanxi* (personal relationship or connections)" frequently appears in western commercial practices and academic journals. A scholar named Stone summarized "It will be impossible for you to live in China without *guanxi*! If foreign negotiators are able to learn game rule, fruitful results will ensue." In China, *guanxi* is so important, but how should one properly maintain *guanxi*?

中国人重视“关系”，建立关系重要，维护关系更重要。当合作告一段落之后，中国人还会努力维护并发展双方的关系，以期维持一种长期、稳定、忠诚的合作关系。在中国，该怎样维护关系呢？

首先，传统节日是中国人维护关系的好机会。人们可以利用庆祝节日的契机，赠送客户礼物，或安排一些娱乐活动，来增进感情。其中，宴请是最传统也是最常见的维护关系的方式，长期以来，中国人很喜欢通过饭桌联络感情、拉近距离。而现在，娱乐活动的形式越来越多样化，舞会、打高尔夫球、唱 KTV 等都是比较受欢迎的活动。

其次，一些特殊时刻也是维护关系的好机会。当合作伙伴有值得庆贺的事时，如生意开张、周年庆典等，如果你能亲自前去捧场，并奉上贺礼，不仅能为对方增光添彩，还能促进双方关系。这种在原有成就上再增添光彩的举动，中国人称“锦上添花”。“锦上添花”会让主人知道你很重视双方的关系。当合作伙伴遇到困难时，如果你能及时提供帮助，将能极大地巩固彼此的关系，因为遇难时的援助远比风光时的捧场重要，也更能体现合

Chinese people stress the importance of *guanxi*. Establishing *guanxi* is important, but maintaining *guanxi* is even more important. When the cooperation comes to a temporary end, Chinese people will strive to maintain and develop the mutual *guanxi* so as to keep a kind of long-term, stable and loyal cooperation. How should one maintain *guanxi* in China?

First and foremost, traditional festivals are wonderful occasions for maintaining *guanxi*. People can make use of the celebration of festivals as an opportunity to send clients gifts or arrange a series of entertainment activities so as to enhance the mutual relationship. Among these activities, entertaining people at dinners is the most traditional as well as commonly seen method of maintaining *guanxi*. For quite a long time, Chinese people enjoyed making friendly contacts and drawing closer from distance at dinner tables. Now, however, the forms of entertainment are becoming more and more diversified, and activities such as dancing parties, playing golf and going to KTV are all highly welcomed.

Moreover, some special occasions are also excellent opportunities for *guanxi* maintenance. When a cooperating partner has something worth celebrating, for example the opening of a business or an annual anniversary, etc., and you can attend the occasion in person and offer your gifts, you will not only enhance the joy and festivity of your partner, but also promote your mutual *guanxi*. This addition of splendor and colorfulness to the existing achievements is referred to by Chinese as "jǐn shàng tiān huā" (embroidering flowers on brocade, meaning adding brilliance to one's present splendor). "Jǐn shàng tiān huā" will let the host know that you value a lot the mutual *guanxi*. When a business partner is confronted with difficulties, if you can offer timely assistance, you will be able to significantly consolidate your mutual

作的忠心。这种在别人生活、工作等方面有难处时提供帮助的行为，中国人称“雪中送炭”。一次“雪中送炭”也许可以促成一辈子的朋友或永久的合作关系。

最后，平日的关系维护也很重要。即便没有什么事，如果你能在平日里打个电话问候一下客户，或者亲自登门拜访，都是维护关系的好办法。如果平时不注重维护关系，只在需要时临时启用，往往被认为是“用得着人朝前，用不着人朝后”、“势利眼”，这在中国是非常为人不齿的。

另外，在中国，维护关系“亦公亦私”，以上这些维护关系的方式，既是在维护商务关系，也是在维护私人关系。中国人喜欢与自己信得过的人合作，维护关系的过程，也是通过各种时机、采取各种办法不断获取对方信任的过程。如果你希望与中国人保持长期稳定的合作，一定要记得在第一次合作以后，就要开始持续不断地维护双方的关系，以求长期、广泛的合作。

guanxi, for assistance when offered in times of difficulty is far more important than flattery given in times of notable success, and can better display one's loyalty for cooperation. This kind of help offered to people who are confronted with difficulties in their life and business is referred to by the Chinese as "xuě zhōng sòng tàn" (offering people charcoal on snowy days). One act of "xuě zhōng sòng tàn" can probably facilitate the establishment of a lifelong friendship and permanent cooperation.

Finally, daily maintenance of *guanxi* is also very important. Even though there are no formal business interactions, you can also give greetings to your clients via phone calls in daily life or visit them personally at their homes. These are all good ways to maintain *guanxi*. If one does not emphasize *guanxi* maintenance in normal times but hopes to immediately use *guanxi* when needed, he/she will be regarded as a snobbish person who "Approaches people when he/she needs them while going away when the need is no longer there". This is taboo in China.

In addition, *guanxi* maintenance in China has "both public and private orientations". The above-mentioned ways of maintaining *guanxi* deal with not only business *guanxi* maintenance, but also personal *guanxi* maintenance. Chinese people like to cooperate with people that they trust. The process of *guanxi* maintenance is also the process of utilizing all kinds of opportunities and adopting various methods to ceaselessly gain the other party's trust. If you hope to keep a long-term and stable cooperation with Chinese, remember to start the continual maintenance of mutual *guanxi* immediately after the first cooperation is over. In this way, one will be able to seek out long-term and extensive cooperation.

案例

刘老是中国教育领域的著名学者，著作等身，成绩斐然。刘老晚年，决定融合自己毕生研究成果，编著一套教材。此举受到业界的广泛关注，各大出版社翘首以待。但刘老的身体状况却每况愈下。有一家出版社打听到这个消息后，马上派专人去照料刘老的生活起居，无微不至，颇得人心。数年后，这家出版社最终获得了这套教材的出版权。

点评 中国人重视维护关系，以求更大的发展。刘老身体不佳，出版社派专人照料刘老，这是在人遇到困难时伸出援手，可谓“雪中送炭”。照顾生活表面看是在维护私人关系，但实际上也是在维护商务关系，亦公亦私。数年的悉心照顾，最终打动了刘老，出版社获得了一次商业契机。

行动指南

- 当双方关系出现裂缝时，本节介绍的维护关系的方式也可用来修复关系。

- 中国人重视已有的关系，人人都有自己的关系网。如果进入了他们的关系网，就要想方设法维护好，有朝一日一旦退出，你想重获信任、再次进入这个关系网的可能性就很小了。

CASE STUDY

As a well-known scholar in the field of education in China, Mr. Liu is prolific in writing and has made remarkable achievements. In his old age, by integrating his lifelong research findings, Mr. Liu compiled a set of textbooks which received widespread attention from the circle. Every major publishing press was on the tiptoe of expectation. However, Mr. Liu's health condition was getting worse and worse. Upon learning this piece of information, one press sent a person to take care of Mr. Liu's daily life. The person cared for Mr. Liu in every possible way and gained his favor. Several years later, the press finally obtained the publishing right of the set of textbooks.

Comments: Chinese people pay special attention to the maintenance of *guanxi* so as to seek for greater achievements. When Mr. Liu was not in a good health condition, the press specially sent someone to take care of him, which means offering help to people who are encountering difficulties. This can be called "Offering people charcoal when it is snowing" (a timely assistance). Taking care of someone's daily life seems maintaining personal *guanxi* on the surface, but actually this is also the like maintenance of business *guanxi*, a combination of business and personal relationships. Years of utmost care finally moved Mr. Liu and gained the press a business opportunity.

ADVICE

- When a fissure appears in the mutual *guanxi*, one can fix it by using the methods of *guanxi* maintenance introduced in this chapter.
- Chinese people value the existing *guanxi*. Everyone has his/her own *guanxi* network, therefore once you step into their *guanxi* network, you should try every possible way to properly maintain it. Once you withdraw from this network some day in the future, chances will be slim for your re-entrance into this *guanxi* network.

同事关系

RELATIONSHIP AT WORK

中国有句话：“天时不如地利，地利不如人和。”（《孟子·公孙丑下》）意思是有利的时机和气候不如有利的地势，有利的地势不如人的齐心协力。中国人崇尚和谐、团结的同事氛围，那么如何处理好与中国同事的关系呢？

There is an old saying in China, which goes as "tiān shí bù rú dì lì, dì lì bù rú rén hé" (*Mencius* · Gongsun Chou II), meaning favorable opportunities and climate are not as important as geographic advantages, whereas, geograpic advantages are not as important as solidarity among people. How to properly handle the relationships with Chinese colleagues since Chinese people advocate a harmonious and united atmosphere among colleagues?

费孝通在《乡土中国》中提到，如果把人与人之间的联系形象化地看作圈子，那么中国人的圈子像是一粒石子投掷在水中，产生层层的波纹。同事关系也像一个圈子，而这个圈子中还有关系远近之分——部门内部、部门之间，合作得较多的人之间、较少合作的人之间，都会形成大小不同、亲疏有别的圈子。规模较大、人数较多的圈子，成员之间的关系就相对疏远一些，对个人融入圈子的要求就低一些；而规模较小的圈子则更需要个人的积极融入；因个人爱好、感情形成的圈子就更要求成员能够主动积极地融入，维持关系。

无论圈子大小，都要求成员要“合群”。所谓合群，是要保证工作上积极配合，更重要的，是要“随和”，不特殊。如果一个人处处特立独行，就会被认为不太合群。另外，中国人常常认为，在工作取得成绩的时候，强调他人的帮助，不突出自己的贡献，也是合群的一个表现。

在中国，同事关系的公私界限不太明显，不仅要求业务上的配合，还提倡情感的投入，交往也未必仅仅止于工作，还可能发展为生活中的朋友。在中国的一些单位里，员工之间的称呼可能并不是全名，不是职位，而是像家里一样称为“哥”、“姐”。当建立起较亲近的关系之后，中国人可能会用对待家人的方式来对待同事，相互交流生活中的事，对彼此表示关心。不仅如此，中国的单位并非全都禁止员工间恋爱，甚至有些

Fei Xiaotong once mentioned in his book *Rural China* that if one looks at the relations among people in a figurative way as circles, the circles of Chinese people resemble the series of ripples caused, by a piece of stone dropping into the water. The relationship between colleagues is just like a circle in which there is a distinction between close relations and distant ones. Whether it is among departments, within a department, or among people who cooperate a lot or seldomly cooperate, there will always be the formation of circles of different sizes and various degrees of closeness. The larger the scale of the circle and the greater the number of its members, the more distant the relationships among these members will be, and the fewer the requirements for individual's integration into the circle will be. For circles with fairly small scale, however, more active participation on the part of individuals is needed. As for circles formed by personal interests and attachment, there are more expectations for members to spontaneously and actively integrate into these circles and maintain the relationship.

No matter how big or small the circles are, members are supposed to "hé qún" (get on well with others or be gregarious). "Hé qún" actually means that people should insure active cooperation in their work and more importantly, appear "amiable" rather than peculiar. If a person shows personal independence of conduct everywhere he/she goes, he/she will be regarded as not quite fitting into the crowd. Besides, when making achievements at work, Chinese people usually believe that it's also a sign of gregariousness for a person to emphasize the help given by others instead of highlighting one's own contributions.

In China, the boundary between public and private in a colleague relationship is not that clear-cut, for the relationship not only requires cooperation in business, but also advocates emotional investment. Moreover, the contact among colleagues may not only be limited to work, they can also develop into friends in daily life. In some working units of China, employees may not address each other by full names or positions, but instead they address each other using "brother" or "sister" as if they belonged to the same family. When a fairly close

典型的中国式单位，还鼓励内部员工恋爱、组建家庭。

因此，中国的公司往往显得其乐融融，氛围融洽。但这也导致有时中国人的制度执行得并不特别严格。中国人向来讲究“礼治”，而非“法治”，倡导“礼”与“德”，认为考虑人情的规定才是合理的规定。因此，他们执行制度的时候常会考虑人情，会通融，常常具体问题具体分析。

relationship is established, Chinese people treat colleagues in the same manner as they treat family members by sharing stories in life and expressing mutual concerns. In addition, employees are not forbidden from falling in love with someone in the same working units in China. Some typical Chinese units even strongly encourage love among their employees and the formation of families among them.

Therefore, Chinese companies are often filled with joy and a harmonious atmosphere. However, this also leads to the relatively less strict implementation of regulations among Chinese. Chinese people have always emphasized "the rule of ethics" rather than "the rule of law" by advocating "courtesy" and "morals", holding that only those regulations taking humanistic elements into consideration can be regarded as reasonable. Therefore, while implementing regulations, they frequently consider human feelings, make exceptions and give particular analysis concerning specific issues.

Nevertheless, there also exists competition among Chinese colleagues. However, people seldom put this kind of competition on the table, thus giving others a superficial impression of colleagues making joint progress in a friendly and harmonious atmosphere.

案例

Elissa与小何是同一个部门的同事，在工作中合作很默契。工作之余，小何经常请Elissa去家里吃饭，并且每次都准备得很丰盛。但是Elissa却从来没有回请过小何。有一次，Elissa过生日，在家里举行生日聚会，邀请了很多好朋友参加，但是没有邀请小何。事后，小何知道了，心中很不高兴，认为Elissa不把自己当朋友，辜负自己平时对她的一片好意。

点评 在中国，同事关系的公私界限不太明显。工作上的默契，让小何跨越工作界线，把Elissa当成很好的私交，并期待Elissa也把自己当成生活中的好朋友。而Elissa却把公私分得很清楚，不会与同事发展私人友谊，因而让小何失望了。

行动指南

- 在中国，关系越亲密的人，越关心对方的个人生活，同事之间也不例外，中国人认为适度的关心并不会侵犯个人隐私。

- 在中国，如果你遇到同事热情地帮你完成工作，请不要介意，在他们看来，这不是越俎代庖，而是关心同事、替人分忧。

CASE STUDY

Elissa and Xiao He are colleagues working and cooperating very well in the same department. When the business is over, Xiao He often invites Elissa to dinner outside and orders a feast every time. However, Elissa has never invited Xiao He. Once, Elissa held a birthday party in her house and invited many good friends except Xiao He. Afterwards, Xiao He learned about the event and felt rather unhappy, for he thought that Elissa doesn't take him as friend worthy of reciprocated kindness.

Comments: In China, there is no clear-cut boundary between public and private in a colleague relationship. The tacit agreement in business causes Xiao He to cross the boundary of co-workers and treat Elissa as an intimate friend. He expects that Elissa will also regard him as a good friend in life. However, Elissa draws a clear distinction between public and private affairs and thus will not develop personal friendship with her colleagues, which eventually disappointed Xiao He.

ADVICE

- In China, people who share a closer relationship will care more about each other's private life. There is no exception among colleagues. Chinese people do not take this as an intrusion of privacy. Rather, they regard it as a kind of concern for others.
- In China, please don't mind when you come across a situation in which your colleagues warmly help you finish your work. In their opinion, it's not an interference with others' affairs, but means caring for colleagues and sharing their worries.

上下级关系

HIERACHICAL RELATIONSHIP

全球性的管理咨询公司 Hay Group 说过：“中国的 CEO 们不太可能给出决策的解释，他们更倾向于发布指令。”中国领导和中国下属有什么特点，又如何处理好上下级关系呢？

Hay Group, a global management consulting firm, once said "Chinese CEOs are unlikely to present strategic explanations. Rather, they are more inclined to give instructions." What are the characteristics of Chinese leaders and their subordinates? How to properly handle superior-subordinate relationships, then?

在中国，平级同事之间相处，比较随和，气氛也很融洽，而不同级别同事之间，尤其是上下级之间，相处一般比较谨慎。中国领导一般很权威，下属以服从领导意见为主，较少提出反对意见或当面辩驳，常常对领导敬而远之。这是因为，在古代，中国人遵从三纲，三纲指“君为臣纲，父为子纲，夫为妻纲”，君、父、夫处于主宰、尊贵的地位，臣、子、妻处于服从、卑贱的地位，三纲强调了对权力的绝对服从，这也成为长期以来人们处理人伦关系、上下尊卑关系的基本法则。至今，等级秩序还在一定程度上影响着职场里的中国人。

中国领导的权威性，让他们在公司或单位里扮演着“一家之主”的角色。工作上的大多数决策，一般都是一位或几位领导决定的，下属一般不参与决策。领导决策之后，一般也不会向员工解释为何做了这样的决策。现在，这种情况有所改变，一些重大决策，领导会征求员工们的意见，但最后拍板的人还是领导。下属也习惯服从领导的决策，较少提出异议。

中国领导不仅在工作上领导他们的员工，甚至在生活上也体现出家长式的关怀。因为，平时上下级关系比较疏远，中国领导如果想亲近员工，通常会采取私下关怀的方式进行沟通，甚至会关心员工的个人生活。在中国人眼里，领导关心下属的个人生活并非侵犯个人隐私，反而这种个别化的关怀更能换取下属的尊敬。而下属也期待团队中能有一个开明而有魄力的领导，在重大事情上能够果断决策。

即便中国领导拥有很高的权威，但是在批评员工的时候，领导还应注意适当维护下属的面子。尽量在批评的时候讲清楚不是针对个人，而是针对事件本身。因为，中国人倾向于把“事”和“人”联系起来，如果批评

In China, colleagues at the same level get along with each other in a rather casual and harmonious atmosphere. However, for colleagues at different levels, namely superiors and subordinates, the communication generally requires more prudence. Chinese leaders are usually very authoritative, and thus subordinates are supposed to obey leaders' opinions in most cases. Subordinates seldom raise objections or make rebuttals face to face, and usually keep at a respectful distance from their leaders. This is because in ancient times, Chinese people obeyed the Three Cardinal Guides which include "Ruler guides subject, father guides son and husband guides wife". Ruler, father and husband were in the predominant and privileged positions while subject, son and wife belonged to the obedient and low positions. The Three Cardinal Guides emphasized the absolute obedience to authority which has long become the basic principle for people's dealing with human relations and relationships between superiors and subordinates as well as between honored and humble ones. Till today, the order of hierarchy still influences Chinese people in the workplace to some extent.

The authority of Chinese leaders accords them the role of "head of the household" in companies and working units. Most of the decisions concerning the work are usually made by one or several leaders, and the subordinates generally do not participate in the decision-making process. When the decision is made, leaders usually won't explain to the staff the reasons why they made such a decision. Now, the situation is changing: for some important decisions, a leader will solicit views from the staff but still act as the person who makes the final decision. Subordinates are also accustomed to obey the leader's decision and will seldom raise objections.

一个人做的事不好就等于批评这个人不好，当面直接指出工作中的错误，就是不给人面子，容易伤害员工的自尊。因此，为了照顾双方的面子，领导更多的是采用比较婉转、含蓄的方式进行批评，有时甚至隐匿于赞赏之中，如 “希望你今后……就能做得更好了”，其实这个“希望”实际上就是批评。

如果你在中国做下属，中国领导会希望你更服从一些；如果你在中国做领导，中国下属会希望你更有魄力一些、对他们更关心一点儿。

Chinese leaders not only lead their employees at work, but also exhibit a kind of parental concern in their daily life. The superior-subordinate relationship is a very distant one in normal times. If a Chinese leader intends to get closer to his staff, he would usually choose to communicate with them in private so as to show his concern for them. He may even care about the private life of his employees. In the eyes of Chinese, a leader's concern for the private life of his employees is not viewed as an intrusion of privacy. Rather, this form of particular concern wins more respect from the subordinates. Meanwhile, the subordinates also expect the presence of an open-minded and formidable leader in their teams who is capable of taking decisive actions concerning important events.

Although Chinese leaders enjoy very high levels of authority, they should nonetheless pay attention to the proper maintenance of their subordinates' face. When criticizing someone, leaders should try to make it clear that the criticism is not directed against individuals, but against the event itself. This is due to Chinese people's association of "things" with "people". If you criticize the poor performance of a person, it amounts to criticizing the individual person for his/her drawbacks. Directly pointing out employees' mistakes concerning their work in front of them is regarded as a sign of not giving face to them, which can easily damage employees' self-esteem. Therefore, in order to save face for the two parties, leaders, in most cases, tend to adopt a more roundabout and implicit manner for expressing criticism. Sometimes, the criticism is even hidden in praise and appreciation, for instance, "hope" in the sentence "I hope you can ... in the future" actually means criticism.

If you are a subordinate in China, Chinese leaders will expect you to be more obedient. If you are a leader in China, your subordinates will expect you to be more bold and resolute and show more concern for them.

案例

Sam 就职于一家中国公司。一天，Sam 去孙经理办公室送文件，在孙经理的办公室遇到同事小马。小马因为下周要做一个手术，正在向孙经理请假。孙经理不仅询问了小马的病情，甚至还就手术的方案给出了建议。Sam 走出孙经理的办公室后，觉得太不可思议了，为什么这么隐私的事情领导都要干涉?

点评 在中国人眼里，领导关心下属的个人生活并非侵犯个人隐私，反而这种个别化的关怀更能换取下属的尊敬。对于孙经理而言，如果明知下属请假做手术，而不闻不问，会显得太冷漠，适度的关心体现了领导对下属的重视。对于小马而言，领导过问自己的私事，是一种特殊的关怀，因此并不避讳。

行动指南

- 如果中国领导询问下属的个人情况，比如“结婚了吗？”“有女朋友了吗？”，请不要介意，他们仅仅是想表达对下属的关心。如果你不愿领导干涉自己的私生活，可以用笑而不答等委婉、含糊的方式回应。

- 如果中国下属事无巨细都向领导请示，并不表示他们没有独立的工作能力，而是为了表达对领导的尊重，他们认为，领导应享有知情权和决策权。

CASE STUDY

Sam works for a Chinese company. One day, Sam goes to Manager Sun's office to deliver some documents and meets his colleague Xiao Ma. As he has an operation coming up in the following week, Xiao Ma is asking for a sick leave from Manager Sun. Manager Sun not only asks Xiao Ma about his sickness but also discusses the operation plan with him. After walking out of Manager Sun's office, Sam feels so difficult to understand why the leader has to interfere with such a private matter.

Comments: In Chinese people's eyes, a leader's concern for the private life of his/her subordinates is not considered as an intrusion of privacy. Instead, this kind of particular concern wins more respect from subordinates. On the part of Manager Sun, if he does not make inquiries when he apparently knows his subordinate is asking for a surgery leave, he would appear too indifferent. However, the timely care displays his high expectations for subordinates. For Xiao Ma, the leaders' inquiry about his private matters is a sign of particular concern, so he does not evade the conversation.

ADVICE

- Please don't mind if Chinese leaders inquire about their subordinates' personal information, for example "Are you married?", "Do you have a girlfriend?", for what they intend to do is only to express their concerns for subordinates. If you don't want leaders to interfere with your private life, you can respond in such tactful and vague manners as smiling without answering, etc.

- If Chinese subordinates ask for instructions from their superiors no matter how important or trivial the matters are, this does not indicate their lack of ability to work independently on their own. Rather, they do this for the sake of expressing respect for their leaders. They believe that leaders should enjoy the right to know and make decisions.

面子

SAVING FACE

知名咨询公司 ClarkMorgan Corporate Training 的创始人之一——Morry Morgan 曾说："许多中国人为了维护他们的好名声宁愿损失利润。" 这里的"好名声"指的就是"面子"，这是中国人极为重视的事情。

Morry Morgan, one of the founders of the famous consulting firm ClarkMorgan Corporate Training, once said that "Many Chinese would rather lose profits in order to maintain their good reputation". Here, "good reputation" refers to "face" which is something Chinese people attach great importance to.

林语堂先生曾形容“面子”、“命运”、“恩典”（Face，Fate，Favor）（林语堂，《吾国与吾民》）为统治中国的三女神。“面子”非常广泛地存在于中国社会中，并且渗透到中国人社会生活的每个层面，是调节人们社会交往的最细腻的标准。中国人爱面子，给不给面子或者面子是否给足，都会直接影响到人际关系的发展，进而决定商业合作是否能够顺利进行。

在社交中，影响中国人面子的因素很多。首先，场合很重要，越是公众场合，在场人数越多，关注自己的人越多，人们越重视自己的面子。比如，人们在商务宴请时要比在办公室里更重视自己的面子。其次，在场者分量越重，或者在场者对自己越重要，人们会越重视自己的面子。比如，人们在领导面前远比在服务人员面前要重视自己的面子。再者，在场者与自己关系越亲近，人们越会重视自己的面子。比如，人们在亲朋好友面前要比在陌生人面前更重视自己的面子。

那么，如何给人面子呢？首先，要多给正面的、积极的评价。越是在重要的场合、关注自己的人越多，在场者越重要、关系越亲近，人们一旦受到肯定、赞赏，越容易获得心理上的满足感和荣耀感。其次，要尽量避免矛盾冲突。中国人喜欢一团和气的氛围，如果在重要场合或当着重要人物的面发生矛盾冲突，是很忌讳的事情，他们也会觉得很没面子。如果矛盾不可避免，不妨找机会私下再沟通，在私密的空间不担心面子问题的时候，中国人会更容易接受你的意见。再者，要尽量避免直接反对或争论，事情遭到反对或者引起争议，中国人常常认为这是对“人”的否定，会觉得没面子，自尊心也会受到伤害。如果不得不提出异议，可以采取委婉、

Lin Yutang once described "face", "fate" and "favor" (Lin Yutang, *My Country and My People*) as the three goddesses governing China. Being widely existent in the Chinese society, "face" has permeated every aspect of Chinese people's social life and serves as the most subtle standard regulating people's social interactions. Chinese people love face very much. Whether a person displays respect to others or whether the respect is adequately shown will directly affect the development of an interpersonal relationship. Further more, it will determine whether a business cooperation can be smoothly carried out or not.

In social interactions, there are many factors influencing Chinese people's face. First of all, occasion is an important factor. The more public the occasion is, the more people who are present, and the more people watching them, the more attention Chinese will pay more attention to their faces. For instance, people will pay to their faces at business dinners than in offices. Second, the more prominent the persons present are, or the more important these persons are to them, the more people will value their faces. For example, people cherish their faces to a considerably greater degree in front of their leaders than before attendants. Moreover, the more closely the persons who are present are related to them, the more people would value their own faces. For instance, people emphasize more their faces in the presence of their relatives and friends than in front of strangers.

How to give face to others, then? First, one should give more affirmative and positive evaluation to people. The more important the occasion is, the more people watching, the more prominent those present are and the closer they are related to each other, people's psychological satisfaction

迂回的方式。

在商务活动中，如何利用面子呢？首先，可以通过给人面子来促成合作。当中国人在熟人面前不好意思讨价还价、斤斤计较的时候，一方面给予积极的评价，给足他们面子，另一方面为自己争取更多的利益。这就是为什么“许多中国人为了维护他们的好名声宁愿损失利润”。其次，可以通过给面子来换取人情。当你不断在众人面前给中国人面子，久而久之，会积累一定的人情。在你需要帮助的时候，可以凭借这份人情来请求他们援助。这个时候，他们碍于面子，只要可以办到的事情，一般不会拒绝。

面子，一方面为中国人赢得尊重和荣耀，但是另一方面可能阻挡他们勇往直前的脚步。现在在中国，往往是敢于“不要面子”的人才能真正做成大事。

and sense of honor will increase in multiples once they are affirmed and praised. Second, one must try to avoid contradictions and conflicts. Chinese people like an atmosphere full of harmony, so it is considered a taboo to provoke conflicts on important occasions or in the presence of prominent figures, for they would feel a sense of disgrace. If conflict is inevitable, one might look for opportunities for private communication. In private spaces where people are not concerned with their faces, it will be easier for Chinese people to accept your opinions. Moreover, one should try to avoid direct opposition or controversy. If things are confronted with opposition or cause controversy, Chinese people would generally regard them as a negation of the individual "person", thus feeling a sense of disgrace and meanwhile affecting their self-esteem. If you have to raise objections, you can adopt an explicit yet roundabout way.

How should one make use of face in business activities? First of all, one can seek benefits by taking advantage of people's love of face. When people feel embarrassed to bargain and argue too much over trivial details in front of their acquaintances, you can give them positive evaluations and show enough face to them on the one hand, and fight for more benefits on your part on the other hand. Many Chinese would rather sacrifice their profits for the sake of maintaining their good reputations which may lead to a advantaged position for a company. Second, you can give face to others in exchange for personal favors. When you continually give people face in the presence of the public, you will gradually accumulate a certain sum of personal favors as time goes on. When you need help in the future, you can ask them for help by using this kind of personal favor. At this point, out of the concern for their faces, people usually won't decline your request as long as it falls within their reach.

"Face" on the one hand wins people's respect and honor. On the other hand, however, it blocks their steps of striving courageously forward. In today's China, people do not like to seek chances for maintaining "face" and lose the company's economic benefits.

案例

一家中国公司近年来业绩低迷，公司 CEO 刘总为了缩减开支，主动提出自降年薪 20%。刘总的好朋友 Nick 听说后建议道：“你可以辞退私人司机，并卖掉公车，这样也能节约开支，何必自降年薪呢？”但是刘总仍然坚持降薪，这让 Nick 无法理解。

点评 如果刘总辞退司机、卖掉公车，周围不知情的人会认为他的职业生涯遭受重大挫折，穷途末路了，这不仅是非常丢面子的事情，也会降低合作伙伴对企业的信心，即便公司情况再艰难，刘总也不能接受。而主动降薪，是一种高姿态，显示出刘总顾全大局的博大胸怀和不计个人小利的无私精神，不仅不丢面子，而且会提升刘总在众人面前的形象，更能鼓舞士气，团结人心，可能让大家同舟共济、渡过困难时期。

行动指南

- 最好不要当众批评中国员工。如果你想纠正一个人的错误，最好是私下里一对一地进行。

- 如果中国人在公众场合出丑了，而又不可补救，他们会觉得很丢面子。此刻，作为旁观者，最好的办法不是上前安慰，而是视而不见。

CASE STUDY

A Chinese company is suffering from an economic downturn in recent years. In order to reduce expenditures, the CEO of the company voluntarily offered to decrease 20% of his annual salary. Manger Liu has a good relationship with the CEO, and one day he found the CEO in private and suggested to him "You can dismiss your personal driver and sell the public car. Then, you can save expenses. It's unnessary to lower your own annual salary." However, the CEO still insisted on his personal wage cut. Manager Liu wondered in his mind: "Why can the CEO be so stupid?"

Comments: If the CEO dismisses the driver and sells the public car, people around who do not know the actual situation would think that his career is suffering from a major setback and that it is reaching a dead end. This would be a very face-losing thing, so no matter how hard the condition of the company is, the CEO cannot accept doing all those things. However, offering to cut his own wages is a high-profile act which displays the CEO as a broadminded person who takes the overall situation into consideration and a selfless man who is not fussy about trivial personal interests. This not only allows him to avoid loosing face, but also enhances the public image of the CEO.

ADVICE

- One had better not criticize Chinese employees in public. If you want to rectify a person's mistake, you'd better do it in a one-to-one private style.

- If Chinese people make a fool of themselves in public settings, they feel very humiliated. At this point, the best thing to do is to pretend that you didn't see it.

社交话题

COMMON TOPICS FOR SOCIAL EVENTS

在商务交往中，谈哪些话题是安全的？又有哪些话题是中国人特别感兴趣的呢？

What topics are safe in business conversation? What topics are the Chinese particularly interested in?

One conversation topic may differ from another as the relationships between the Chinese are different. The topics are determined by the closeness of the relationships: topics are different between the family members and acquaintances, someone you are only slightly acquainted with and someone you have only first met.

中国人的人际关系有远近亲疏之别，因此人与人之间谈论的话题也是有区别的，家里人之间的话题与熟人不同，熟人与点头之交不同，点头之交与初识之人也不同。

对于初次见面的陌生人，人们喜欢谈论彼此的姓氏和家乡，以此拉近距离。中国当前使用的姓氏有4000余个，据分析，使用人数排名前100个姓氏的人口占全国总人口的84.77%。排名前五位的是"王、李、张、刘、陈"，这几个姓氏人口均多于2000万。中国有一句俗语"五百年前是一家"，意思是"同姓之人，上祖本是同一宗族"。这种说法虽然并不准确，但如果人们发现对方与自己有相同的姓氏，会倍感亲切，彼此的心理距离会拉近。除了姓氏之外，初次见面的人还喜欢谈论家乡。中国地域广阔，来自相同地域的人，口音、习惯、性格、喜好也趋于一致，因此也会让人彼此有亲近感。这种地域的概念可大可小，小到同一个村、同一个乡，大到同一个省，或者同一个地理区域（如东北三省）。在外地遇到自己的"同乡"，常常感到相互之间存在着"亲情"，以至于"老乡见老乡，两眼泪汪汪"。在聊天中还有这样的现象：虽然双方不是同乡，但一方曾经到过对方的家乡或对那里有一定的了解，甚至认识从那里来的人，都会提出来和对方聊一聊，引起共鸣。借由姓氏和家乡，双方会从陌生变得渐渐熟悉起来。跟人聊一聊共同关心的天气、交通状况，比如感叹一下天气晴好、交通顺畅，或者共同抱怨一下忽然变冷、变热、交通拥堵等，也会让人迅速找到共同话题。

对于有些许了解但却并不熟悉的双方来说，他们会选择一些令人轻松愉快、身心放松的话题。比如休闲娱乐、电影电视、音乐、风土人情、烹饪小吃、天气、四周环境等；或者格调高雅的文学、艺术、哲学等话题；也可能是与工作有关的某些细节，例如职业、任职时间、职业

When meeting a stranger for the first time, people like to talk about their surnames and hometowns to get a closer relationship with each other.

There is a classic text named *The Hundred Family Surnames* (Chinese: 百家姓, containing more than 400 surnames) in China. According to analysis, the people with the first hundred surnames account for 84.77% of the national population. The top five surnames are "Li, Wang, Zhang, Liu and Chen," each owning more than 20 million people. There is a Chinese saying that "500 years ago, we were in the same clan", meaning the people with the same surnames are the descendants of the same clan. Although this argument is not reliable, a person will feel close to the one he talks with when he finds he/ she has the same surname with him. That means that the distance in the hearts of the two people will be shortened. Besides surnames, people like to talk about their hometowns when they first meet each other. Since China is a vast country, people from the same region may feel close to each other for having similar accents, habits, characters and interests. The region could be as small as a village or a particular countryside area, or be as large as a province or a geographic area, such as the "Three Northeast Provinces (consisting of Heilongjiang, Jilin and Liaoning provinces)" in China. It says that "If a person meets a fellow villager in other provinces, he may often feel a sense of kinship and his eyes may even be moist with tears". If they are not fellow villagers, one will usually tell the other one that he has been to his hometown or knows something or somebody in his hometown, hoping to arouse a resonance between them. By talking about surnames and hometowns, the two strangers will gradually be familiar with each other.

If the two sides are slightly acquainted, they will choose very relaxing and happy topics, such as entertainment, film, television programs, music, local customs and culture, cooking, snacks, weather, surrounding environment, etc. Elegant literature, art, philosophy and other topics are also included. And the details of work, such as profession, office time and vocational interests may be mentioned as well. But the personal interests will not be involved in the conversation. Everyone feels free to speak out his/her opinions and everyone will have something to

兴趣；等等。这些话题不涉及谈话双方的切身利益，人们可以各抒己见，发表自己的看法，人人都有话可说。如果有相同的兴趣爱好，可以因此建立良好的朋友关系。因此如果想和对方成为好朋友，不妨主动引出上述话题，对方通常会给予积极回应，免不了有一番热烈、顺畅的长谈。

在熟人之间，谈话是非常有针对性的，甚至不避讳彼此的年龄、收入、恋爱婚姻状况、家庭、儿女等私事。这是因为中国人认为熟人之间理应对对方表示关心，考虑对方的所思所想，而这些“私事”是与他们的生活关系最密切、最重要的，所以应该有所了解。有的人还愿意主动与别人分享这方面的情况，以示亲近和对别人的信任，表明“我们都是自己人”。因此，如果遇到有中国人问及一些“私密”话题，请不要觉得被冒犯，很有可能你已经被划入“熟悉的朋友”这个圈子内，他们只想表达对你的关心和重视。

当然，话题也依不同年龄、不同性别的交谈对象而不同，这需要适时而变，但总而言之，应选择对方喜欢、感兴趣的话题。据一项调查表明：男人在一起主要谈工作、体育等，较少说起家庭生活与家庭成员；女人在一起说得更多的是家庭，如孩子、家务等。因此，在商务交往中，如果谈话对象是异性，为了迎合对方的兴趣，让交际顺利和谐地进行下去，不妨有意识地选择让对方有兴致开口的话题。比如同女人谈谈家庭、孩子，同男人说说工作、体育。

总之，选择合适的话题，可以帮你结识更多的朋友，而有了一张社交关系网，商务活动的开展一定会更加顺畅。

say. If you have the same interests or hobbies with a person, you may build up a good relationship with him and might be his friend. If you want to be someone's good friend, you'd better bring up the above subjects. In general, you will receive positive responses followed by a passionate and long conversation.

The conversation between acquaintances tends to focus on some specific topics, even involving some private affairs such as age, income, boyfriend or girlfriend, marriage, family and children. It is considered as a common thing to show care to someone you know well and to understand that man's thoughts by knowing his personal affairs since these affairs are the closest and most important things in his life. Some would like to share private information with others without asking. That's because they want to get close to you and show their trust to you as well as indicate that you are "one of their closest friends". Therefore, if you are asked about some private affairs by the Chinese, don't feel offended because maybe you are just being brought into the circle of "acquainted friends". You should remember they just want to show care and great attention to you.

Of course, the topics may differ as the speakers change. It is necessary to find a proper topic when talking with people of different ages and genders. In short, you should choose the topic that the other side will like or be interested in. According to a survey, men like to talk about work and sports rather than family life and family members when they get together, while women regard the family such as children and housework as the most popular topic. As a result, in business conversations, if you meet someone of the opposite sex, you'd better choose some topics that may satisfy his/her curiosity and he/she prefers to talk with you, thus making a successful and happy conversation. For example, as a man, you can talk about family and children with a female partner. As a woman, you can talk about work and sports with a man.

To sum up, a proper topic will help you make more friends. When you establish a social network successfully, it will be easier to do business in China.

案例

王颖是中国某高校的女教授，一次赴英国某高校讲课。在机场，王教授见到了一直和自己有邮件往来的英方院长 Stinson 教授。Stinson 教授对王教授的到来表示欢迎，并称赞她年轻有为，在学术研究方面取得了杰出的成绩。王教授微笑着解释说："我已经不年轻了，今年都五十多了。"王教授的回答让 Stinson 教授惊讶不已，中国女士怎么会如此不避讳自己的年龄呢?

点评 中国人并不认为年龄是一个很私密的话题，特别是在已经认识了一段时间的朋友之间。因为年龄增长不全意味着"变老"，它还代表了丰富的人生阅历和经验。年长的人更值得尊敬，所以对中老年人来说，并不避讳谈年龄。此外，当别人夸中年以上女士相貌年轻时，她们有可能主动报告自己的实际年龄或是让对方猜测自己的岁数，最期待听到下一句是"你看起来一点儿也不像是这个岁数"。这样，她们会有一种满足的心理。

CASE STUDY

As a professor in a Chinese university, Mrs. Wang Ying went to a British university to give a lecture. At the airport, Professor Wang met the dean of the British university----Mr. Andre, who had kept in touch with her by e-mails. Mr. Andre showed warm welcome to her and praised that she had made outstanding achievements in academic research at such a young age. "I'm not young any more. I'm more than fifty", Wang replied with a smile. Andre was surprised to hear that, and he begun to wonder why this Chinese lady felt comfortable to make no secret of her age.

Comments: For the Chinese, age is not a very private topic, especially among the friends that have known each other for a period of time. The reason is that age is not merely a number. It represents how rich one's life experience is. Since seniors win more respect, it is not a taboo for the middle-aged men and elders to talk about their age. When someone praises a women of middle age or above stating that she looks younger than others of the same age, she will usually tell you her real age or let you guess her real age. In either circumstance, you should say "You completely don't look your age!" to fulfill her expectation. Only by doing this will the lady be satisfied.

行动指南

- 在商务交往中，应避免以下话题：政治话题、国家的历史遗留问题（如台湾问题），与商业无关的中国共产党和政府的政策，涉及国家、行业机密的话题，用民族习惯开玩笑的话题。这些话题有的容易引起意见分歧，有的会让人心生戒备，这都可能会让双方不欢而散。

- 大多数受过高等教育的中国人在与外国人交往时，都会尊重他人隐私。但万一因为对方表达关心而被问到不想回答的问题，你可以绕开话题或让对方猜一猜，还可以笑着说“这是秘密”。一般情况下，中国人都会表示理解，并且不会再继续追问下去。

ADVICE

- There are topics that should be avoided during business conversations such as politics, national secrets, or any other sensentive issues that may hurt the feelings of the Chinese people. Some of the topics may lead to disputes, and others may make others defensive, all of which might result in a parting in discord.

- When talking with foreigners, most highly-educated Chinese will respect their privacy. But in case they are driven by curiosity and ask you some questions that you don't want to answer, you can change a topic or let them take a guess, or just say "It's a secret" with a smile. Generally, the Chinese will get the point and will not persist.

节假日
HOLIDAYS

在中国，节假日不仅仅是休息、娱乐的日子，也是很好的商机，还是建立和维护商务关系、表达对员工的关怀的好时机。

In China, festivals and holidays are not only for people to take a rest and be entertained, but good opportunities for doing business. It is a good time to establish and maintain business relationships, as well as to care about employees.

节日是一个民族文化中最精致、最具代表性的部分。中国文化的开放性和包容性使得中国的节日构成也呈现出缤纷多彩的特点，有传承了几千年而积淀下来的传统节日，如春节、端午节、中秋节等；有近代以来产生的有国际意义的节日，如劳动节、儿童节等；有从西方传入的节日，如圣诞节、情人节等。这些节日都受到了商家的重视，成了促销、宣传的契机。

在这些节日中，传统节日最好地体现了人与自然的关系，它既是中国人长期不懈地探索自然规律的产物，包含着大量科学的天文、气象和物候知识，也是中华文明的哲学思想、审美意识和道德伦理在民俗风情上的集中体现。每个传统节日都有不同的文化内涵，也都有相关的物品和活动作为载体，对商家来说，这些传统节日为他们提供了无限商机。一些外国商家就开发出了本土化的节日商品，例如美国的冰激凌品牌哈根达斯就针对中秋节开发了冰激凌月饼。

除了传统节日，近年来西方节日越来越受追捧，这与商家的炒作有很大关系。在这些节日中商家促销造势程度最高的当属情人节。在这一天，情侣都不愿放弃展示爱情的机会，衣服、鲜花、化妆品、珠宝首饰等热销，巧克力店、电影院、公园等在这一天也极为热闹。商家都想方设法将自己的商品与情人节挂钩。近年来，不只是青年男女，中老年夫妻间过情人节的也越来越多。

正是看重了“爱情经济”这个卖点，中国版的情人节——“七夕节”也逐渐升温。七夕起源于汉代，又名乞巧节，是纪念古代神话中的织女的节日，旨在女子祈求智慧与技艺。然而，商家们却另有想法，这一天，消费成了表达爱情的主要方式，借着牛郎织女的传说，从鲜花到巧克力，甚

The festival is the most delicate and most representative part of the Chinese culture. The Chinese festival is characterized by its great variety, which contributes to the openness and inclusiveness of the Chinese culture. Some of them are traditional festivals that have thousands of years of history, such as the Spring Festival, the Dragon Boat Festival, the Mid-Autumn Festival, etc. Some are modern festivals which are of international significance, such as Labor Day, Children's Day and so on. Some are introduced from western countries, such as Christmas, and Valentine's Day, etc. Besides the festivals mentioned above, there are festivals created by businessmen, such as Singles' Day, Chinese Valentine's day and so on.

Among these festivals, traditional festivals best embody the relationship between man and nature. Chinese people persisted in exploring the laws of nature, leading to the creation of the traditional festivals containing a large amount of scientific knowledge concerning astronomy, meteorology and climate. The Chinese philosophy, aesthetic consciousness and moral ethics are also embodied in the folk customs of these festivals. Every traditional festival has its own cultural connotations, as well as its own items and activities to show these connotations. As for the businessmen, they have gained infinite business opportunities from these festivals. Some foreign companies have developed products that are suitable for the local market. For example, the American ice-cream brand Haagen-Dazs made the ice-cream moon cake particularly for the Mid-Autumn Festival.

Besides the traditional festivals, western festivals are becoming more and more popular in recent years, and this has much to do with commercial speculation. Valentine's Day is the most highly promoted western festival in China. During the festival, lovers are reluctant to give up the opportunity to show their love, so clothes, flowers, cosmetics and jewelry are sold well and chocolate shops, cinemas, parks and other places are bustling with excitement. Every shop is trying to connect its products with the Valentine element. In recent years, not only young men and women, but also an increasing number of middle-aged and elderly men are beginning to celebrate Valentine's day

至到上千元的“萤火虫套餐”，商家挖空心思地兜售浪漫，七夕节传统的纪念方式正被新方式日渐取代。

在为商家带来商机的同时，节日也是建立和维护商务关系的好时机。中国人讲究“礼尚往来”，这里的礼不仅有“礼物”的意思，更是一种礼仪、仪式和道德程序。节日期间亲戚、朋友、邻居之间互相拜访、馈赠礼品，由此加深了彼此之间的联系，拉近了彼此之间的距离。在所有节日中，春节尤其受到中国人的重视，是一年中最喜庆和令人期待的日子。只要是祝福性的拜访，人们都不会拒绝。人们从内心深处是敞开的，乐于接受祝福与问候，这是其他节日不具备的特性。在喜庆的氛围下人们都很友善，是一年中绝好的与客户交流的时机。需要注意的是，这个时段拜访客户一定是要错开中国农历正月初一到初三，这三天中国人一般都要探亲访友或有另外重要的安排。可以在这之前或之后，预约一个时间带着礼物登门拜访。

除了向合作伙伴表达节日祝福，节日也是给员工发放福利、体现关怀的好时机。每逢节日，网上各大论坛晒福利的帖子都备受追捧。节日前夕为员工发过节费（或购物卡、商场购物券）、提前放几个小时的假、送节日礼品（以大米、食用油、水果为代表）是大多数企业采取的方式。因此，除了休假，福利也是大家对节日充满期待的原因之一。

自从中国步入信息化时代，节日祝福也有了新的形式，发送精美的电子贺卡，特别是发祝福短信成为节日间你来我往的手段之一。以2013年春节除夕当天为例，短信发送量高达133亿条。亲人之间、朋友之间、同事之间都互发短信，表达感激和祝福。在网上也很容易找到各种祝福“模板”，

with their wives.

Since the selling point "love economy" is appealing to businessmen, the Chinese version of Valentine's day---- the "Qixi Festival (Seventh Day of the Seventh Lunar Month)" is becoming more and more popular. This festival, also known as the Qiqiao Festival, has been celebrated since the Han dynasty to commemorate Zhinv stemming from ancient mythology. During this festival, girls would pray for wisdom and skills. However, it seems that businessmen have different ideas. They think consumption is the major way to show love on this day. The legend of Niulang (the cowherd, symbolizing Altair) and Zhinv (the weaver girl, symbolizing Vega) was used to sell products. From flowers to chocolates, even to the "firefly package" that is worth thousands of RMB are all sold in this festival. Consequently, the traditional way of celebrating Qixi is being marginalized.

Festivals not only bring business opportunities to the businessmen, but also create a good chance to establish and maintain business relationships. Chinese people think highly of the saying "Li Shang Wang Lai (礼尚往来, "礼" which refers to etiquette and courtesy rather than gifts)" which means "etiquette requires reciprocity". During the festivals, relatives, friends and neighbors will visit each other and present gifts to each other to deepen the understanding of both sides and to shorten the distance between the two sides. Among all the festivals, the Spring Festival is regarded as the most important festival in China. It is the happiest event and most appealing festival of the year, and visits for giving blessings will be welcomed during this festival. People open their heart and will be glad to accept blessings and greetings, which does not happen in other festivals. Since people are immersed in delightful atmospheres, it is an excellent time to communicate with clients. But you should remember to avoid visiting clients from the lunar New Year's Day up until the third day of the lunar year. Because these three days are often considered as days to visit relatives and friends or to do other important activities. Therefore, it would be better to contact the host in advance and then visit his house with a gift before or after these days.

It is a proper time to express

如蛇年祝福短信——“蛇腾喜浪迎新纪，龙乐丰仓送旧年”。短短的信息在收发间温暖着彼此的心，也让节日变得更有人情味。

good wishes to cooperative partners, and show care for employees by giving benefits during the festivals. Once the festival comes, forum posts in every big BBS showing the benefits the employees gained are quite popular. Most enterprises will distribute a festival bonus (or in the form of gift cards or shopping vouchers) to their employees before the festival. Or, they will give a couple of hours off in advance, or give festival gifts (often rice, edible oil and fruits) to the employees. Therefore, besides the day-offs, the benefits and gifts are another reason that people look forward to festivals.

Since China entered the information era, new forms of festival greetings began to prevail. Sending exquisite e-cards and sending text messages in particular, have been the most common way to express blessings. For example, the number of text messages sent on the lunar New Year's eve of 2003 was around 13.3 billion. Relatives, friends and colleagues send text messages to each other to express gratitude and blessings. It is easy to find all kinds of blessing "templates" on the Internet, such as a text messages welcoming the Year of the Snake: "She Teng Xi Lang Ying Xin Ji, Long Le Feng Cang Song Jiu Nian (蛇腾喜浪迎新纪，龙乐丰仓送旧年)". Although the message is short, it warms the hearts of both the sender and receiver, thus making the holiday more heartwarming.

案例

都说中国的春节是最重要的节日，也最热闹。为了体验热闹的“中国年”，2012 年 Mike 特意留在北京过春节。可没想到的是春节期间北京的人少了，车也少了，许多店铺也都关门了，路上显得比往日冷清了许多。Mike 不明白为什么中国最热闹的节日却如此冷清？他回想起一个多月前的圣诞节倒是更热闹一些，节日气氛甚至比他的家乡还要浓厚。

点评 在中国，有数以亿计的人口在离家较远的大城市工作，春节是全家团圆的日子，为了回家过春节，大批人口从北京、上海、广州等大城市乘坐各种交通工具返家，形成大量的人口流动。以 2012 年为例，春节期间离开北京的人口约 900 万。因此，Mike 会感到春节期间的北京比平时冷清一些。而圣诞节，中国人口不会大量流动，反倒是商家促销的好时机，商家会举办各种庆祝活动，十分热闹。

CASE STUDY

It is often said that the Spring Festival is the most important and liveliest festival in China. In 2012, to enjoy the lively Chinese New Year, Mike decided to stay in Beijing during the Spring Festival. But unexpectedly, there were fewer people and cars during the festival. Many shops were also closed. It seems that the streets became sleepier than ordinary days. Mike didn't know why the city was so quiet during the liveliest festival in China. He remembered that one month ago that Christmas was more exciting and the festival atmosphere in Beijing was stronger than that in his own country.

Comments: In China, the Spring Festival is an occasion for the family to get together. To go home and celebrate this festival, a large number of people will return to their hometowns from Beijing, Shanghai, Guangzhou and other big cities by various means of transportation, leading to a significant shift in population. In 2012, for example, about 9 million people left Beijing during the Spring Festival. Therefore, it is reasonable for Mike to have felt more desolate than usual in Beijing. During Christmas, there will be no massive population flow. Instead, it would be an excellent time for the business owners to promote their products and hold various activities. So it will be very exciting during Christmas.

行动指南

- 中国大陆法定节假日合计有11天。分别是：元旦1天，春节3天，清明节1天，劳动节1天，端午节1天，中秋节1天，国庆节3天。一般在放假时国家会考虑与临近的双休日一块儿安排休息，也就是“串休”。

- 在中国南方沿海地带，除了年终奖以外，领导在春节后还会向员工派发开工“利是”（“红包”在粤语区的叫法），取其凡事顺利的意头，且每封开工“利是”内附一张心意卡，印上勉励词句，以激励员工。派出的“利是”少则几元，多者也不超过50元。每名员工都一样，不与业绩挂钩，代表着一份关心，以增加员工对公司的归属感。

- 春节期间，中国会出现“全民大迁移”的现象。人们在节日到来前纷纷踏上返乡之旅与家人团聚。每年春节前后有40天是客流最集中的时间，被称为“春运”。2012年末的春运，往返客流超过了30亿人次。在大城市，除了上述现象，法定节假日的前一天下班高峰期通常最为拥堵。因此，要合理安排出行时间，尽量避免与节日“移民”撞车。

ADVICE

- There are 11 days in total amongst the official public holidays in mainland China, including 1 day-off for New Year, 3 days-off for the Spring Festival, 1 day-off for the Qingming Festival, 1 day-off for Labor Day, 3 days-off for the Dragon Boat Festival, 1 day-off for the Mid-Autumn Festival, and 3 days-off for the National Day. Generally, the government may borrow a nearby weekend to make a given holiday longer, which is referred to as "Chuan Xiu" in Chinese.

- In the coastal area of southern China, other than the year-end bonus, leaders may hand out "Li Shi" ("red packets" or cash-filled envelopes called "Li Shi" in Cantonese, because "Li' means 'Everything goes well") to the employees after the Spring Festival. There is also a blessing card containing encouraging words in every envelope. Although the money is not much, ranging from several Yuan to less than fifty Yuan in different companies, the employees in the same company receive the same amount of money as it has nothing to do with their performance. It is just a gift to the employees in order to show care and promote their sense of belonging to the companies.

- During the Spring Festival, you may witness a "national shift" in China. People depart for their hometowns before the festival. The 40 days before and after the Spring Festival are considered as the peak passenger flow period, also known as the "Spring Rush". In 2012, during the Spring Festival, the number of round trip passengers exceeded 3 billion. In big cities, besides the above phenomenon, the most congested time would usually come at the evening rush hour before the official public holidays. Therefore, it is necessary to arrange a reasonable travel time to avoid encountering the festival "population shift".

图书在版编目 (CIP) 数据

商务社交 /《中国商务文化》编写组编著. —北京：北京语言大学出版社，2013.12（2016.12 重印）
（中国商务文化）
ISBN 978-7-5619-3715-0

Ⅰ.①商… Ⅱ.①中… Ⅲ.①商务－礼仪－商务－中国－汉、英 Ⅳ.F718

中国版本图书馆CIP数据核字（2013）第295328号

书　　名：商务社交
SHANGWU SHEJIAO
责任编辑：王墨妍
责任印制：陈　辉

出版发行：北京语言大学出版社
社　　址：北京市海淀区学院路15号　邮政编码：100083
网　　址：www.blcup.com
电　　话：编辑部　8610-8230 1016
国内发行　8610-8230 3650/3591/3648
海外发行　8610-8230 0309/3365/3080
读者服务部　8610-8230 3653
网上订购电话　8610-8230 3908
客户服务信箱　service@blcup.com
印　　刷：北京建宏印刷有限公司
经　　销：全国新华书店

版　　次：2014年1月第1版　2016年12月第3次印刷
开　　本：889毫米×1194毫米　1/16　印张：4.75
字　　数：79千字
书　　号：ISBN 978-7-5619-3715-0 / F・13304
定　　价：196.00元（含DVD）